CONTEMPORARY WEDDING SONGS

CONTENTS

— PIANO LEVEL —
LATE INTERMEDIATE/EARLY ADVANCED

ISBN 0-634-07428-8

HAL•LEONARD®
CORPORATION
7777 W. BLUEMOUND RD. P.O.BOX 13819 MILWAUKEE, WI 53213

Visit Hal Leonard Online at
www.halleonard.com
Visit Phillip at
www.phillipkeveren.com

PREFACE

Finding the perfect wedding music can be both a joy and a challenge. This collection was assembled to help in that task. Featuring popular favorites from several decades, we hope this folio will provide just the right song for each special moment in your wedding ceremony.

Two compositions of a personal nature are also included. When Lisa and I were married in 1985, I composed "Prelude for Lisa" to serve as the processional. This was a magical moment in our life together, and we hope that other couples will enjoy the piece as well. When our friends, Andy and Janet Medley, were married in 1996, "Northwoods Wedding" was our wedding gift to them. Their wedding weekend was set in the inspiring beauty of a northern Wisconsin summer, and this composition was written in anticipation of that scenic location.

If you are searching for traditional material, I would like to recommend the companion to this folio, *Classic Wedding Songs*. This collection features perennial favorites that have graced ceremonies for generations.

Sincerely,
Phillip Keveren

BIOGRAPHY

Phillip Keveren, a multi-talented keyboard artist and composer, has composed original works in a variety of genres from piano solo to symphonic orchestra. Mr. Keveren gives frequent concerts and workshops for teachers and their students in the United States, Canada, Europe, and Asia. Mr. Keveren holds a B.M. in composition from California State University Northridge and a M.M. in composition from the University of Southern California.

FOREVER AND EVER, AMEN

Words and Music by PAUL OVERSTREET
and DON SCHLITZ
Arranged by Phillip Keveren

4

GIVE THANKS

Words and Music by
HENRY SMITH
Arranged by Phillip Keveren

To Coda ⊕

HERE, THERE AND EVERYWHERE

Words and Music by JOHN LENNON
and PAUL McCARTNEY
Arranged by Phillip Keveren

NORTHWOODS WEDDING
for Andy & Janet

Composed by PHILLIP KEVEREN

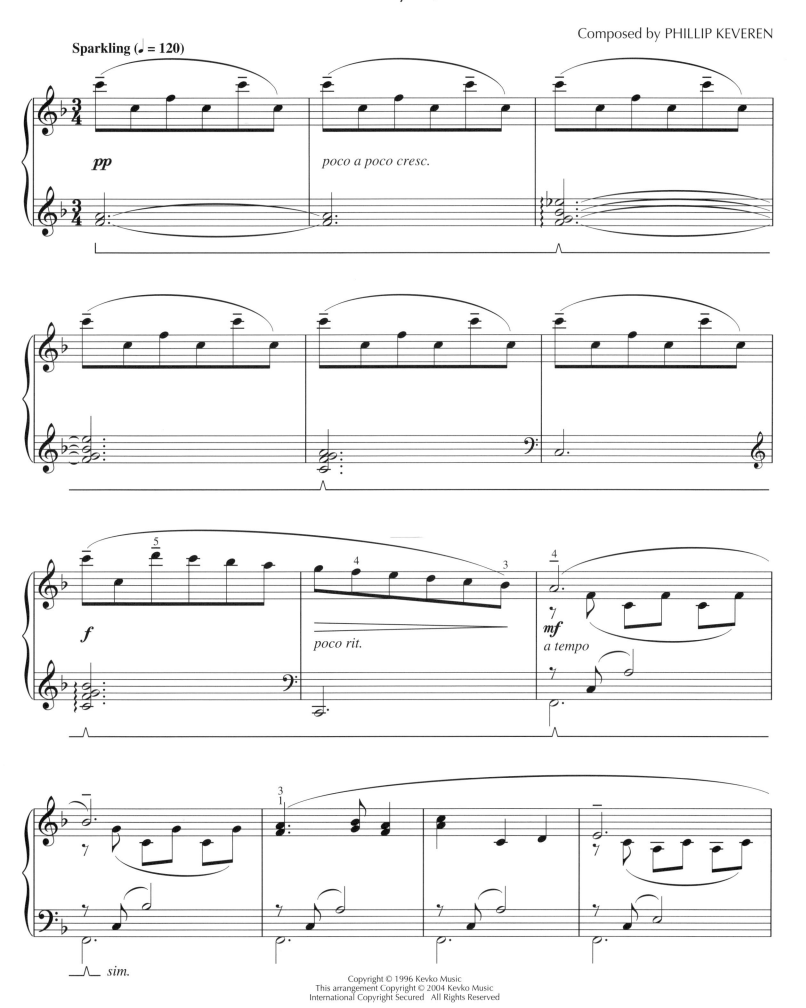

Slightly slower, tenderly

p a tempo

HOW BEAUTIFUL

Words and Music by
TWILA PARIS
Arranged by Phillip Keveren

With tenderness, freely expressive

I WILL BE HERE

Words and Music by
STEVEN CURTIS CHAPMAN
Arranged by Phillip Keveren

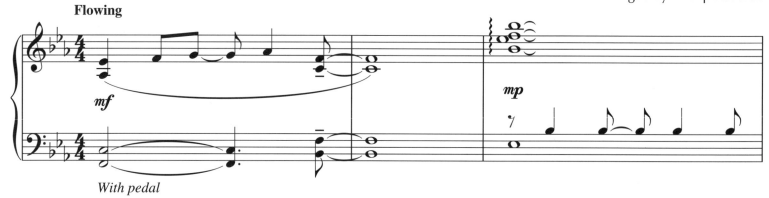

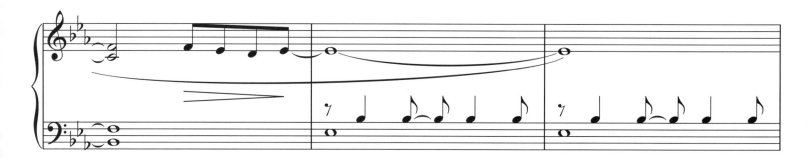

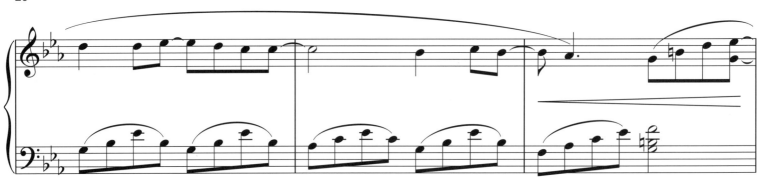

D.S. al Coda

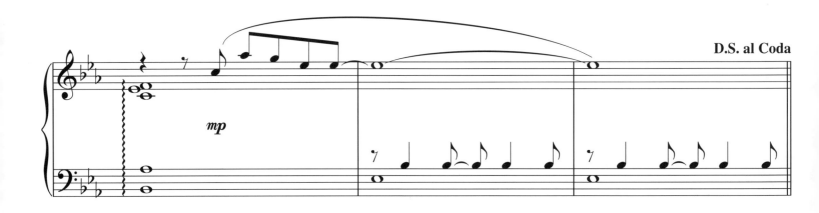

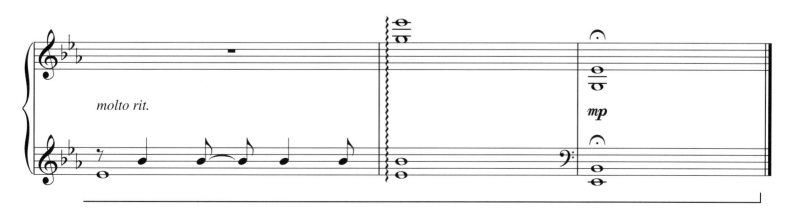

IN THIS VERY ROOM

Words and Music by RON HARRIS
and CAROL HARRIS
Arranged by Phillip Keveren

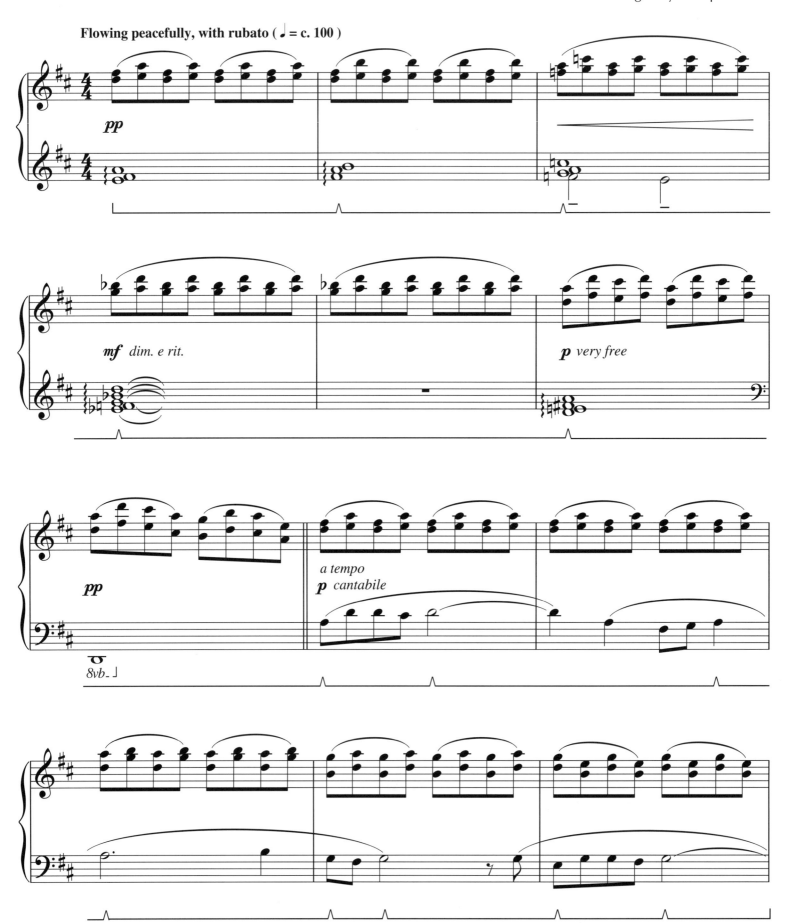

LONGER

Words and Music by
DAN FOGELBERG
Arranged by Phillip Keveren

THE LORD'S PRAYER

By ALBERT H. MALOTTE
Arranged by Phillip Keveren

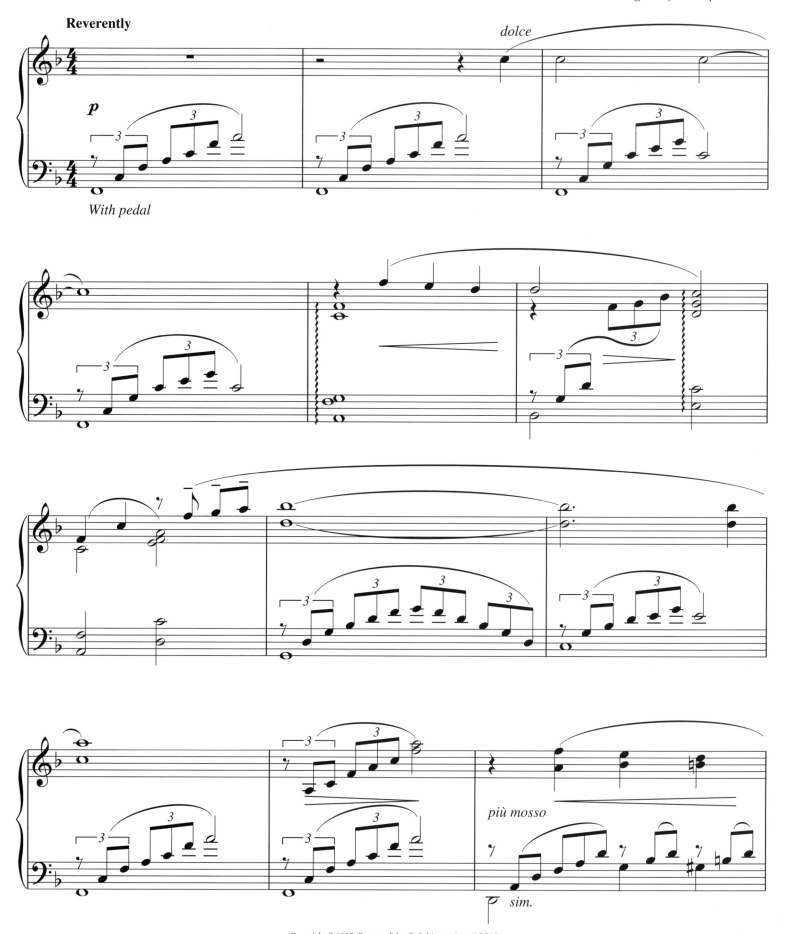

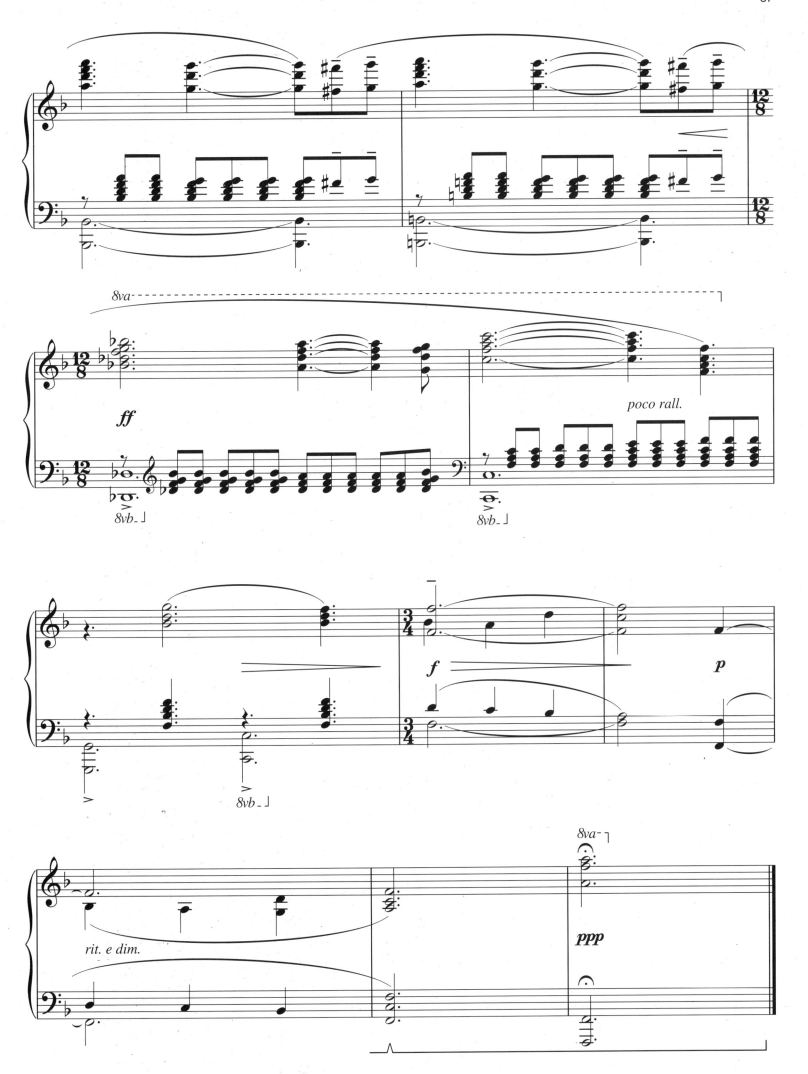

LOVE WILL BE OUR HOME

Words and Music by
STEVEN CURTIS CHAPMAN
Arranged by Phillip Keveren

Flowing gently

With pedal

Slowly, freely

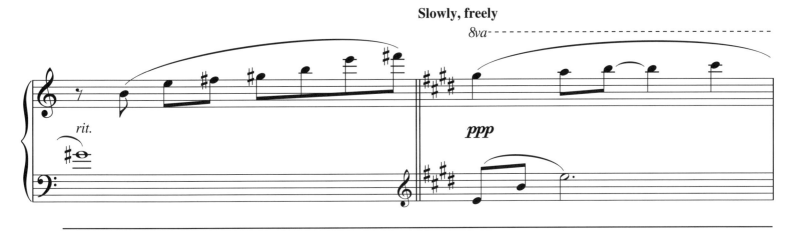

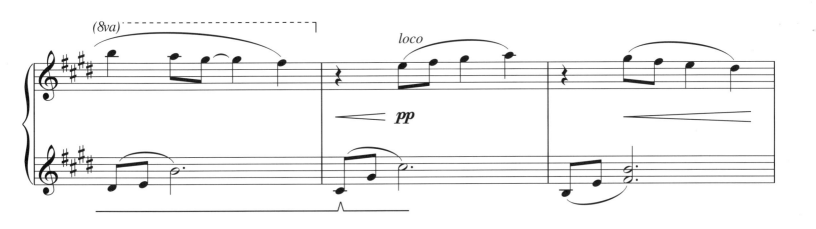

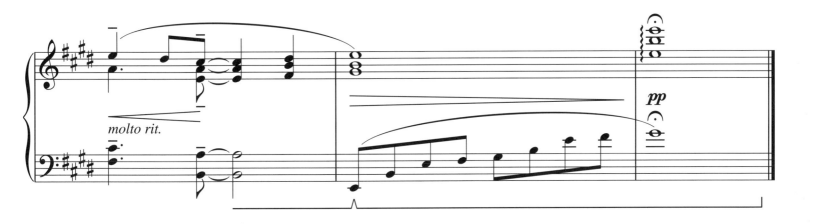

PRELUDE FOR LISA

Written by
PHILLIP KEVEREN

D.S. al Coda

UNCHAINED MELODY
from the Motion Picture UNCHAINED

Lyric by HY ZARET
Music by ALEX NORTH
Arranged by Phillip Keveren

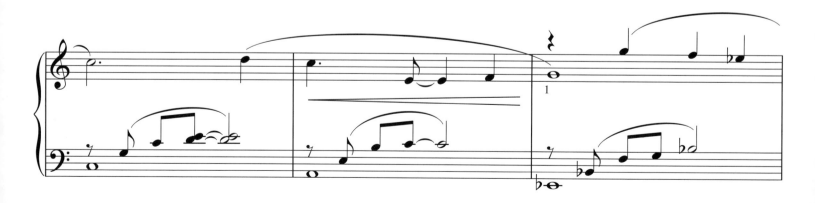

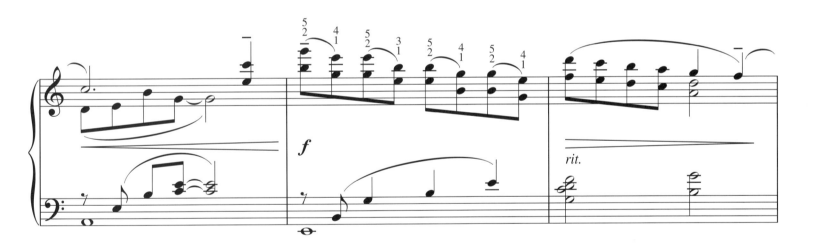

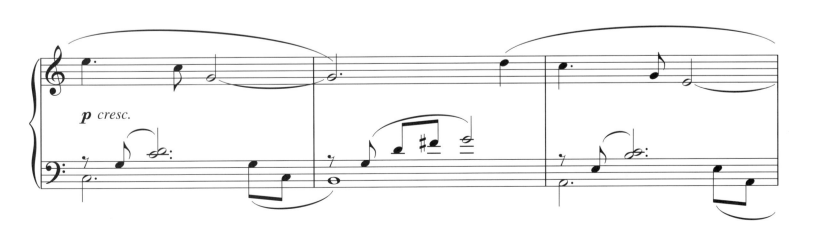

To Coda ⊕

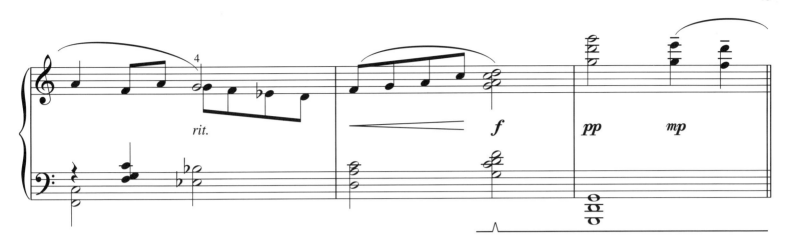

Tempo I

D.S. al Coda

CODA

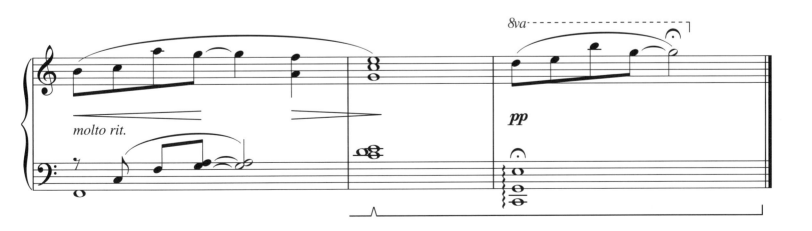

VALENTINE

Words and Music by JACK KUGELL
and JIM BRICKMAN
Arranged by Phillip Keveren

Tenderly

WE'VE ONLY JUST BEGUN

Words and Music by ROGER NICHOLS
and PAUL WILLIAMS
Arranged by Phillip Keveren

WEDDING PROCESSIONAL

from THE SOUND OF MUSIC

Lyrics by OSCAR HAMMERSTEIN II
Music by RICHARD RODGERS
Arranged by Phillip Keveren

With fanfare

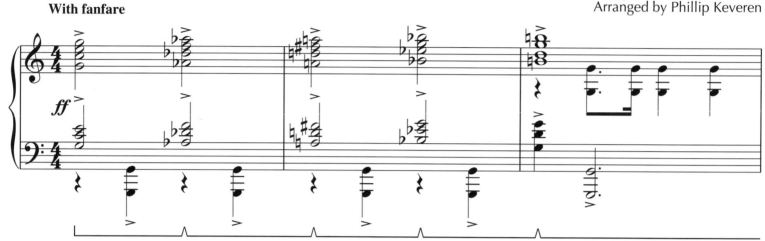

Stately March

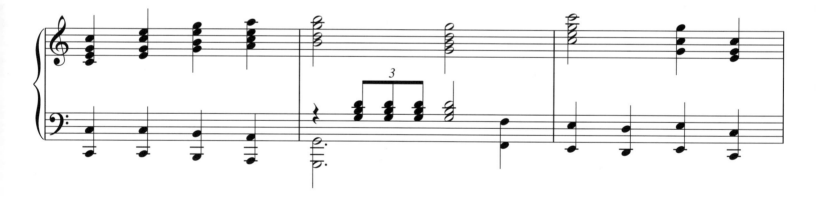

YOU'LL NEVER WALK ALONE

from CAROUSEL

Lyrics by OSCAR HAMMERSTEIN II
Music by RICHARD RODGERS
Arranged by Phillip Keveren

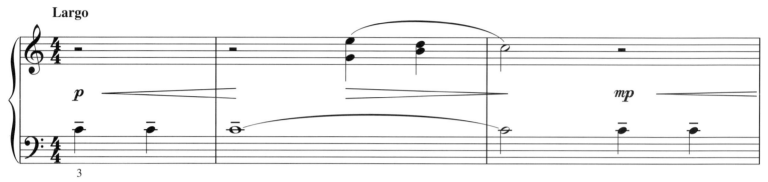

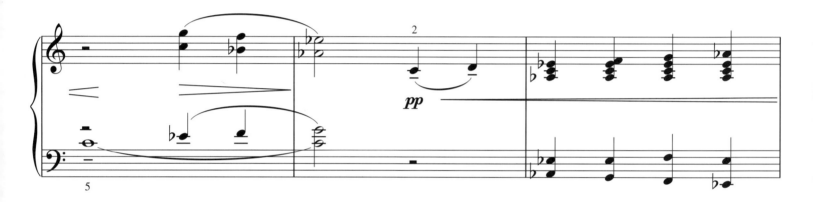

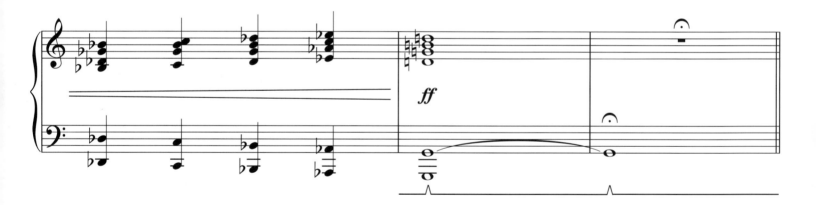

Andantino molto cantabile

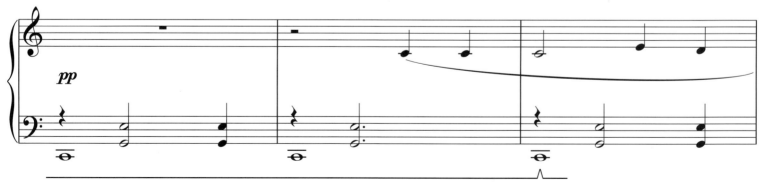

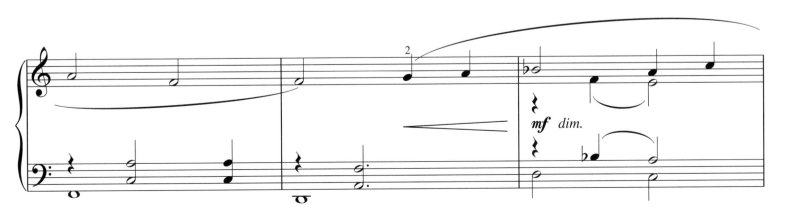

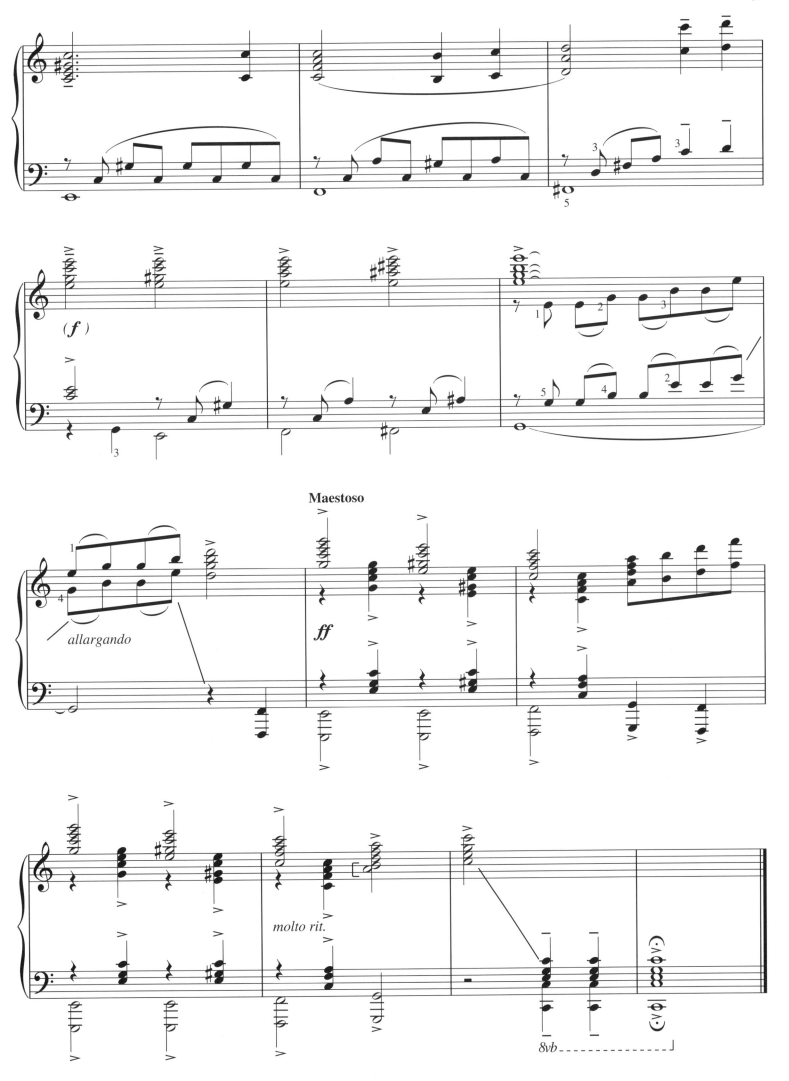

WHEN I FALL IN LOVE

Words by EDWARD HEYMAN
Music by VICTOR YOUNG
Arranged by Phillip Keveren